I SPY
Shapes in Art

For Walter and Molly

FOREWORD

Introducing children to art is so simple – it only takes a few pictures – but the rewards are endless for both parent and child. Artists have been around for thousands of years and the work they have left behind gives us a unique record of how they lived and thought. This fantastic legacy is unrivalled as a source of pleasure and wisdom. Art can make us laugh or cry. It can open our eyes to things we never noticed before. It can stir us into action or make our spines tingle. Anyone can join in, and with a child as a guide it is even more fun.

Look for the shape I have chosen in each of these paintings and then find other shapes with which to play 'I Spy'. Talk about them, count them, compare them. There are colours to think about too and small details to spot. Some children might like to make up a story around a favourite picture, some might have fun copying one. Anything goes. Just one of these activities allows enough time for a picture to be filed away in a child's memory, and that is what this book is all about.

Lucy Micklethwait 2004

Cover picture: Auguste Herbin, *Composition on the Word 'Vie', 2*
Title page picture: Paul Klee, *Around the Fish*

I SPY
Shapes in Art

Devised & selected by Lucy Micklethwait

Collins

An imprint of HarperCollinsPublishers

I spy
with my little eye

a square

Wassily Kandinsky, *Soft Hard*

I spy
with my little eye

a circle

Winslow Homer, *Blackboard*

I spy
with my little eye

a rectangle

Henri Matisse, *The Snail*

I spy
with my little eye

a triangle

David Hockney, *Self Portrait with Blue Guitar*

I spy
with my little eye

a semicircle

Georgia O' Keeffe, *Ladder to the Moon*

I spy
with my little eye

an oval

Paul Klee, *Around the Fish*

I spy
with my little eye

a diamond

Joaquín Torres-García, *Form, Structure and Objects*

I spy
with my little eye

a heart

Fernand Léger, *Composition with Hand and Hats*

I spy
with my little eye

a red star

Peter Blake, *Some of the Sources of Pop Art*

I spy
with my little eye

a cylinder

Andy Warhol, *Big Torn Campbell's Soup Can (Pepper Pot)*

I spy
with my little eye

a cube

Joe Tilson, *Nine Elements*

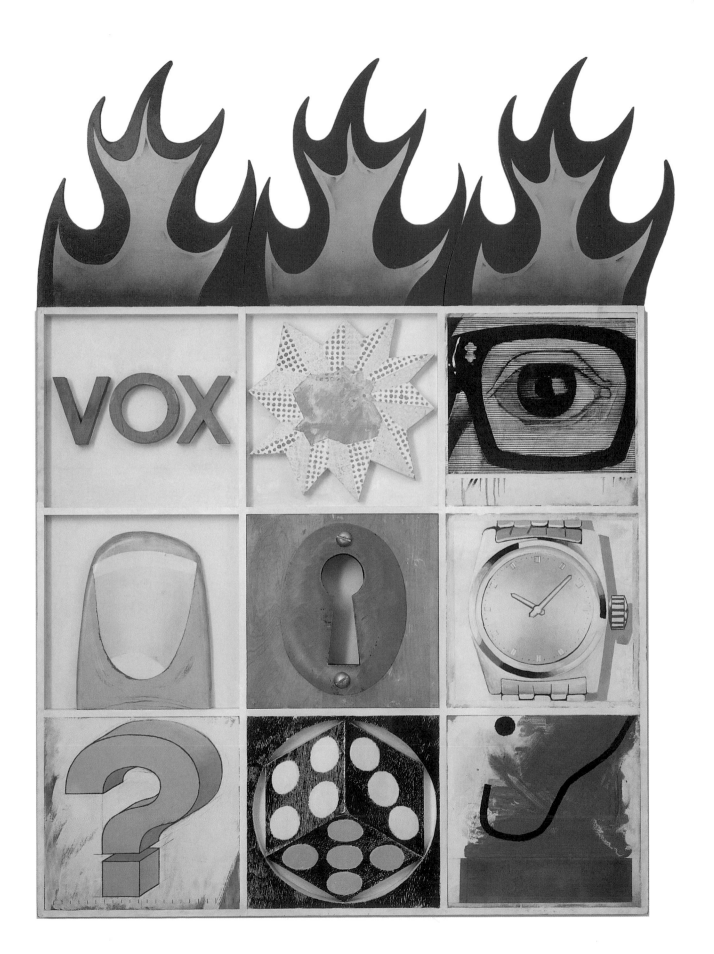

I spy
with my little eye

a cone

René Magritte, *The Promenades of Euclid*

I spy
with my little eye

a sphere

M. C. Escher, *Hand with Reflecting Sphere*

1-35 MCE

I spy
with my little eye

ten circles

What do you spy?

Auguste Herbin, *Composition on the Word 'Vie', 2*

— I Spied With My Little Eye —

Square
Wassily Kandinsky (1866-1944), *Soft Hard* (1927)
Fondation Maeght, Saint-Paul de Vence

Circle
Winslow Homer (1836-1910), *Blackboard* (1877)
National Gallery of Art, Washington, D.C.
Gift of Jo Ann and Julian Ganz, Jr.

Rectangle
Henri Matisse (1869-1954), *The Snail* (1953)
The Tate Gallery, London

Triangle
David Hockney (born 1937), *Self Portrait with Blue Guitar* (1977)
Private Collection

Semicircle
Georgia O'Keeffe (1887-1986), *Ladder to the Moon* (1958)
Collection Emily Fisher Landau, New Mexico

Oval
Paul Klee (1879-1940), *Around the Fish* (1926)
The Museum of Modern Art, New York

Diamond
Joaquín Torres-García (1847-1949), *Form, Structure and Objects* (1943)
Private Collection

Heart
Fernand Léger (1881-1955), *Composition with Hand and Hats* (1927)
Musée National d'Art Moderne, Centre Georges Pompidou, Paris

Red Star
Peter Blake (born 1932), *Some of the Sources of Pop Art* (2000)
Private Collection

Cylinder
Andy Warhol (1928-1987), *Big Torn Campbell's Soup Can (Pepper Pot)* (1962)
The Andy Warhol Foundation, New York

Cube
Joe Tilson (born 1928), *Nine Elements* (1963)
Scottish National Gallery of Modern Art, Edinburgh

Cone
René Magritte (1898-1967), *The Promenades of Euclid* (1955)
The Minneapolis Institute of Art
The William Hood Dunwoody Fund

Sphere
M.C. Escher (1898-1972), *Hand with Reflecting Sphere* (1935)
Escher Foundation, Gemeentemuseum, The Hague

Ten Circles
Auguste Herbin (1882-1960), *Composition on the Word 'Vie', 2* (1950)
The Museum of Modern Art, New York
The Sidney and Harriet Janis Collection

ACKNOWLEDGEMENTS

The author and publishers would like to thank the galleries, museums, private collectors and copyright holders who have given their permission to reproduce the pictures in this book.

Wassily Kandinsky, *Soft Hard*, © ADAGP, Paris and DACS, London 2004. Photograph Bridgeman Art Library

Winslow Homer, *Blackboard*, Gift (partial and promised) of Jo Ann and Julian Ganz Jr., in Honour of the 50th Anniversary of the National Gallery of Art. Photograph © 2004 Board of Trustees, National Gallery of Art, Washington

Henri Matisse, *The Snail*, © Succession H Matisse/DACS. Photograph © Tate London 2004

David Hockney, *Self Portrait with Blue Guitar,* © David Hockney

Georgia O'Keeffe, *Ladder to the Moon*, © ARS, NY and DACS, London 2004. Collection Emily Fisher Landau, New Mexico (Amart Investments LLC)

Paul Klee, *Around the Fish*, © DACS 2004. Digital Image © 2004 The Museum of Modern Art/Scala, Florence

Joaquín Torres-García, *Form, Structure and Objects*, © ADAGP, Paris and DACS, London 2004. Photograph © Christies Images Ltd 2004

Fernand Léger, *Composition with Hand and Hats*, © ADAGP, Paris and DACS, London 2004. © Photograph CNAC/MNAM Dist RMN/Jacques Faujour

Peter Blake, *Some of the Sources of Pop Art,* © Royal Academy of Arts, London. Peter Blake 2004. All Rights Reserved, DACS

Andy Warhol, *Big Torn Campbell's Soup Can (Pepper Pot),* © The Andy Warhol Foundation for the Visual Arts, Inc./ARS, NY and DACS London 2004. Trademarks licensed by Campbell Soup Company. All Rights Reserved. Photograph © The Andy Warhol Foundation, Inc./Art Resource, NY

Joe Tilson, *Nine Elements*, © Joe Tilson 2004. All Rights Reserved, DACS

René Magritte, *The Promenades of Euclid*, © ADAGP, Paris and DACS, London 2004

M.C. Escher, *Hand with Reflecting Sphere*, © 2004 Cordon Art B.V. - Baarn - Holland. All Rights Reserved

Auguste Herbin, *Composition on the Word 'Vie', 2*, © ADAGP, Paris and DACS, London 2004. Digital Image © 2004 The Museum of Modern Art/Scala, Florence

First published in Great Britain by Collins Picture Books in 2004

3 5 7 9 10 8 6 4
ISBN: 0-00-713133-X

Compilation and text copyright © Lucy Micklethwait 2004

Collins Picture Books is an imprint of the Children's Division, part of HarperCollins Publishers Ltd.

The HarperCollins website address is: www. harpercollins.co.uk

Printed and bound in Singapore

Other titles in the series

I Spy – An Alphabet in Art
I Spy – Animals in Art
I Spy – Numbers in Art
I Spy – Transport in Art